I0840998

AFFINITY OR MISERY

by Karen Kellock Ph.D.

Manual for Superior Men

**A complete theory based on Einstein physics,
Political Psychology, Systems Theory
and Archetypal Psychiatry.**

FORMULA

**All success attraction
All disease obstruction
All recovery elimination**

You must fast on all three

OBSTRUCTIONS:

**People
Habit
Food**

AFFINITY OR MISERY

Friends love you on your way down but in your winning season they're not around. A shameless brutal psychopath you keep forgiving convinces you'll be happy with him. When I met her she sized me up, looked me up and down and hated me like an mean dog. Like a war survivor I got the right perspective and secluded with God. When I woke up to the game, the matrix, the system I was a new person: the cure is education.

BE WISE TO BE MADE RICH

GOD CAN'T MAKE YOU RICH UNTIL
GOTTA GROW UP TO HANDLE BLESSINGS
GOD GAVE IT TO YOU NOT THEM
MONEY IS A BAROMETER OF MATURITY
POCKET WATCHING & ENTITLEMENT
THEY REALLY HATE YOUR GUTS
BE NOT IGNORANT: SATAN'S DEVICES
SEE THEM THEN DON'T LIKE EM
PRAY FOR THE *WHOLE* ARMOR
BE HARMLESS BUT WISE
GOD GIVES IT TO TEACH LESSONS
MONEY IS A MAGNET
THEY DON'T UNDERSTAND WHY GOD DID IT
PRAY TO MAINTAIN IT
PRAYER IS BETTER THAN GIVING MONEY

BE WISE TO BE MADE RICH

The bible says God wants to prosper us but we block His beautiful blessing by letting people use us.

GOD CAN'T MAKE YOU RICH UNTIL

God won't make you rich til He can trust you with finances. You've been too good to deceiver spirits.

Ask God to order your steps with the kind of success He has over your life. Users always cause strife.

God can't trust you with money He blesses you with if you buy want you want not what you need.

As soon as He blessed me those scammers would come in and I'd be a "good hostess" with them.

Everyone wants to separate a fool from his money It's hard to hold onto it til you've had this journey.

I was easily scammed then had PTSD for years over it. I had to get STRONG/vehement to hold onto it.

It makes me sick looking back when such a wallflower. Don't feel guilty for not lending, ever!

How can God bless you with your DESTINY of having money if you lend it out so dam easily?

I was so good to the hobosexual always fixing him dinner. Then he'd ask for money, what a scammer.

Women are taught to give in. We're PRIMED to be used and discarded like an old shoe, good to them.

GOTTA GROW UP TO HANDLE BLESSINGS

BE WISE TO BE MADE RICH

Hide your money when you get it cuz everyone wants some of it plus the goodies you buy with it.

Until you're strong [like a velvet gove] how can God pour His many money blessings into you Love?

The hobos in your life just take, take, take. You're constantly giving until you finally grow up ok.

GOD GAVE IT TO YOU NOT THEM

If you GIVE TOO MUCH God won't finally bless you with your wonderful destiny which is to be RICH.

Stop saying you're "generous". That's just a cover for the fact that you're weak, always giving too much.

Every saint has a past, every sinner has a future. That's how it is so ignore the insults of accusers.

They push you into misery while promising joy. It's the justice of the conquerors who love to destroy.

A criminal mentality can overtake a nation. This social psychology should really fascinate you son.

But as sure as God, black and white: what's done in the dark will be brought to the light. Johnny Cash

Once you see it's all about money and they want yours honey you finally deserve God's blessing see.

MONEY IS A BAROMETER OF MATURITY

They feel entitled to it. Since you are friends, relatives or grew up together you OWE THEM/must lend.

This is the main reason you must relocate then find friends just as rich lest you can't hold onto it.

BE WISE TO BE MADE RICH

What you gonna do when they hit you up for $500 cuz they know you have it? Can you say NO to it?

Money matters: cuz it's a sign of maturity knowing how to handle it. Your **FINANCES**: God is viewing it.

It's the same with workers. Are they collaborators or mere takers? Must find/court trusted workers.

You must be **READY** for the takers and scammers. This also is a sign of your readiness as God pours.

I was such a fool for "friends" I lent out many thousands once. He never paid back a penny to this dunce.

I couldn't handle being called "selfish". I'd wince when all I had to do was close the door in their face.

The hippy new age would downplay the importance of money but now I see it as **THE** sign of maturity.

The most important word in the vocab is 'NO!" for God's watching when you give to moochers below.

POCKET WATCHING & ENTITLEMENT

Be very careful of people constantly pocket-watching you. They have their eyes on your wallet Sue.

These people feel entitled to the blessings God has given you. Aren't you sick of this Sue?

You may even want it, thinking they'll be more loyal. I was like this, their plans I didn't dare foil.

They'd even say "I know you've got it, come on". That's how you know they feel entitled to it son.

The truth of the matter is: you don't have to do a thing for **NOBODY**. We grow up & see this in maturity.

BE WISE TO BE MADE RICH

I'd cringe when I saw it coming. Like I had to give it to them or I'd be an obvious selfish, greedy nobody.

You can TELL when people are jealous of you, always throwing shade on your divine success too.

They advise you, laugh with you and even feed you but the truth is they ENVY you so don't be fooled.

Then want what you possess. When envious of success you don't know it because they don't show it.

If apprehensive of their next request it's better to get rid of these moochers and uninvited guests.

THEY REALLY HATE YOUR GUTS

Deep down in their spirit they hate your guts. Recognize jealousy comes from Satan and lower pits.

When blessed, pray to God "keep me safe from all my enemies" cuz they want what's in your wallet.

This is why you must LOVE your enemies so God can make em your footstool with you not the fool.

You love em from a distance but not a firm handshake cuz you know the devil wants your money ok.

You're high up in the spirit. You come with good graces and they're argumentative so now you know it.

When you pray for success God gives you finances but also elevation in the spirit your highness.

When someone's rich so is their aura. They can feel you're very wealthy, they can see it Sarah.

They can see you're rich by how you carry and conduct yourself, in your submission to God/fear of hell.

BE WISE TO BE MADE RICH

If you remain a fool, how can God trust you with money? Think on this then understand the wait see.

They see how you love people/how humble you are with the presence of God, so they want your wad.

BE NOT IGNORANT: SATAN'S DEVICES

Be not ignorant concerning Satan and his device. Keep your head above water and get free of lice.

Just as you train a puppy not to be into everything, you gotta watch people cuz it's the same thing.

Just cuz God blessed you don't start showing off. It's a trigger for the scammers but it defies God.

"Lord I need you to order my steps today & send Your angels to protect me from thieves/robbers ok?"

People will do everything in their power to take your success from you. Humans have two sides Sue.

Having money is an orientation. You know all want it from you and you walk tall in your station.

The more successful you become the more people's true colors come out and you see the bums.

SEE THEM THEN DON'T LIKE EM

The more money you make the more you see: you don't like these people anymore then you're FREE.

Money may not buy happiness but money IS happiness: you're so alive and excited now your highness.

You aren't happy busted and disgusted. The bible says money is the answer to all things, believe it.

BE WISE TO BE MADE RICH

Just cuz you have money doesn't mean you should be messing with everybody and every thing.

Money DOES put you on a high plane, the separation between you and them is obvious now ok.

Get rich & wonder why the hatred now. It's not they don't wanna see you good but better than them: wow!

Get a trusted financial advisor [sister, friend] and direct all moochers to them, that's how you lend.

PRAY FOR THE *WHOLE* ARMOR

You must pray for the whole armor of God because people will switch on you. They'll turn Sue.

The more you give to them the more they won't love you, just your hand. That's how it works man.

When they're envious of you they couldn't care less about your heart. It's Satan doing his part.

God has now given you power but never forget money is the root to all evil when it comes to people.

Stay obedient and humble and always abide in the ord of God esp. when he makes you successful.

When you pray for success pray for everything that comes with it. Lord keep it in my wallet.

BE HARMLESS BUT WISE

This is why you're harmless as a dove but wise as a serpent. Esp. for you women, be adamant.

When some people get money they change, getting a haughty prideful spirit. This often may ruin it.

BE WISE TO BE MADE RICH

I was very young when God gave ti to me before. I didn't pray and it departed and went afar.

Huge amounts of money were spent unwisely: I had holes in my bucket. It happens, be sure of it.

You get heady when you have a buncha money. Satan says you need something when you don't honey.

When I easily lost the money God was preparing and shaping me for later, for when I had far greater.

GOD GIVES IT TO TEACH LESSONS

When God gives you something knowing you can't handle it He'll have it taken, to learn from it.

He'll have it taken just to teach you a lesson: don't trust those evil friends, stay tight man.

When people show their true colors, believe em. They may apologize but never forget that lesson.

When you make money again, love em from a distance but don't ever get close again my friend.

Love people from a distance but guard your favor. God gave it to you not your relatives and neighbors.

Keep your guard up and don't let anyone get too close to you. Any of yor associates will do it Sue.

"Lord make me wealthy, take me to the next level" should include: "keep me safe out here too".

MONEY IS A MAGNET

Money is like a magnet and they're very clever planning how to get it. Separate from maggots.

BE WISE TO BE MADE RICH

When praying you must rebuke envy, jealousy and **ENTITLEMENT**. Pray for these things see.

No one believes in you when you're struggling & have nothing but **NOW** they believe? Be careful honey.

When you're successful everyone wants to ride with you but their hand is out so **WATCH OUT**.

Everyone wants to break bread with you, they all wanna spend time with you. It's tempting Sue.

Don't ever forget that when you were losing they all wanted to lose you. They dumped you too.

Now they all have "opportunities" for you to make money. Don't engate with this, it's still envy.

THEY DON'T UNDERSTAND WHY GOD DID IT

They don't understand how your God made you so successful. They're just envious of it all.

You are blessed & highly favored but to them you don't deserve it despite being such a hard worker.

They wail: "lord why did you choose him and not me?" They shake their fist then target you see.

Now God gave you the big bag/planted your feet on higher ground their true colors come out now.

New money is a spiritual thing. Everyone can't go with you man, get that through your head darling.

Stop trying to bring everyone with you to the next level. It's very tempting to be the head honcho.

Stop breaking bread with people who'd never break bread with you. When broke they were gone Sue.

BE WISE TO BE MADE RICH

Stop giving people all your time when they never had time for you back in the day when so blue.

A fool and his money will soon depart. And you worked hard for your success from the start.

You worked hard for this breakthrough, just to give it all away? Learn to say NO and keep it ok.

PRAY TO MAINTAIN IT

Once you have it, pray to MAINTAIN success. That's the trick of all this, don't lose it again sis.

Don't ever forget that what God did for you, He did it for YOU. You don't owe anyone a thing Sue.

People left you for dead and counted you out. Now you have money they all want what you got.

They won't reveal they know you're a success but always have their hand out, beggars no less.

They can't support you but constantly got their hand out. I tell you, block em all, beggars and louse.

Envy and jealousy is REAL. When you pray for success pray for all that comes with it like raw deals.

If a man doesn't work he won't eat. You did the work and they didn't but still they beg for your money.

PRAYER IS BETTER THAN GIVING MONEY

Instead of giving em money, pray for them with words of encouragement. Keep to this/be adamant.

All you give will be motivation, inspiration and a prayer. You're righteous so it avenges much I declare.

BE WISE TO BE MADE RICH

Those who feel entitled to blessings God gave you will be gone if you ever hit bottom again, amen.

Pray for success & elevation but also everything that comes with it: remember this always or lose it

Pray against those pompous spirits who are jealous of what you have but not willing to work to get it.

Satan roams around seeking who to devour at this time. Getting money opens a can of worms, aye.

When successful you'll be meeting spirits of manipulation and guile. See them as spirits not people.

BULLIES AND MISERY

JEZEBEL'S HIT MEN
BIGGEST BLOCK TO FEMALE GENIUS
RIDICULE IN GROUPS/TOWNS
UNDERHANDED WOMEN
SOMETHING YOU DID ONCE
NO LOYALTY
COMING HOME TO SELF
EMPTY TEENS AND MEAN GIRLS
ESCAPING FEMINISTS/LIBERALS
GOOD MARRIAGES: AFFINITY
INHERITED SHAME
DESTINY
OTHER PEOPLE KEEP US DOWN
REWARDS OF OVERCOMING
THIS RELATIONSHIP IS DEVASTATING
ALCOHOL AND THE DEVIL

BULLIES AND MISERY

Beauty ideals, persecution and silencing: true in the middle ages for women but also today see.

You can't raise a little man to be a big man with character. He'll be a sneak till he's down under.

Never announce your departure before leaving the narcissist. He'll block or resist/don't be a fool sis.

They'll strip your financial resources so you can't escape to a new place. Think: SILENCE lady.

Be strategic and calculated before taking your steps in your field. Always think: everyone's evil.

It's a situation of life or death. You must be thinking/preparing or it's a rough road ahead.

JEZEBEL'S HIT MEN

Don't worry about sister, that backstabber got exactly what she deserved from God my Father.

The wicked get hit men for their dirty work. Jezebel won't kill but her friends cause disaster still.

The wicked things she SAID instigated hatred even riots against you and your loved ones too.

While appearing innocent she bashed you so behind your back til your whole world collapsed.

She's an expert at sly innuendo, lighting fires while appearing innocent. That's Jezebel each minute.

BULLIES AND MISERY

She was the alpha female in town surrounded by her flying monkeys/little women hanging around.

While professing friendship she gossiped constantly making me an ostracized slave see.

I existed on the sad fringes until husband brought me back to reality about the liberal witches.

There is nothing crueler as these queen bees get their gophers to do their bidding: without mercy.

This system of "her hit men" is far more dangerous than one angry man, it is unrestrained bedlam.

Beware of women for even the churchwoman will go to war on the odd girl out refusing to conform.

BIGGEST BLOCK TO FEMALE GENIUS

The biggest obstacle to female genius is not the males but the female community itself: it is hell.

Things may have been different in the fifties and this may be a postmodern perspective, agreed.

Inconvenient women were burned as witches and don't forget it was other women who were snitches.

Strange women were put in concentration camps due to the gossip dossier from the female ranks.

Any odd girl is the instant target of women colluding against her--a fixed action pattern of fakers.

20,000 French women collabs shaved bald: how much of that was scapegoat revenge I asked God.

My Dad always said: "Hold your head up HIGH". He knew of the undertow against queens, aye.

BULLIES AND MISERY

Conform or be killed, ostracized, hated, jilted or fired. Narcissist moms are the worst/most dire.

Women are so ruthless in collusive calumny I had to relocate like a parachute taking me to safety.

In my new home I was instantly surrounded by nice people in a safe area in conservative America.

RIDICULE IN GROUPS/TOWNS

In small towns you're ridiculed wherever you go. Word travels fast cuz they love to hate ya' know.

It's hard to find a church for solace either. The false church is everywhere: heresies of the secular.

The only thing for this sickening, gut-wrenching situation is go within/pray to God your Friend.

Make plans to escape these people. A contagious madness trapped you but God frees us of evil.

They get on the horn and roundup a posse against you. Your life and goals destroyed/you're screwed.

Men and I had the same persecutors: WOMEN. I shudder recalling when ruled by them.

She collects allies while bashing you besides. The sheriff is her sidekick, groomed to despise.

UNDERHANDED WOMEN

Women don't know how to fight so they fight DIRTY. By getting groupies riled up against one see.

The female genius ends up with no female friends nor males but if happily married she won't fail.

BULLIES AND MISERY

Born sovereign the world breaks her down right away. Walking into final success she's exhausted ok.

History's been cruel to women, I know. But the current level of female-hatred is just as bad and low.

Coming under the tyranny of a woman is worst. They're compelled to torture you right at the first.

Godly females know what I'm talking about. They don't resent these truthful words nor does God.

Nothing is more frustrating than coming under the tyranny of a female like that: I'm still healing.

Not to say men are any better, I've come under ruthless sadists looking innocent: it's similar.

SOMETHING YOU DID ONCE

They'll peg you for something you did once and call it your lifestyle. They'll incite riots against you gal.

Once rid of jezebel, never her let her in again. For she takes advantage after worming her way in.

I let her back in once, forgiving soul that I am. She destroyed me twice over/created bedlam.

For she has the devil in her, working thru division. She'll split your family up, she'll kill your pets son.

The minute she gets an edge, she takes over. This is her main characteristic, don't forget it ever.

NO LOYALTY

The godly female takes pride in loyalty but most switch sides when it suits their purposes see.

BULLIES AND MISERY

Some jealous evil old women become cruel persecutors with age and then these harridans die ok.

Realization: Some cruel older women jealously hate younger females and will even beat them up.

Cindy, the sacred cow in town, controlled the whole gestalt with gossip: her MAJOR WEAPON.

COMING HOME TO SELF

Does a narcissist mom thrive on creating rivalry? Yes, the golden child becomes her chosen bully.

The brilliant body screams "run to the hills and don't look back" cuz they wanna use you: fact.

Healing from abuse is incomplete without reconnecting to your intuition: that's the true self kicking in.

This is a joyous homecoming: not to be "best" but to finally be your SELF after losing it to hell.

Reconnecting to your voice: if a predator shows up again you listen to the body and get away fast.

Your body is your biggest asset when fighting the narcissist for it is superior in detecting lies.

EMPTY TEENS AND MEAN GIRLS

Empty teenagers going along with the crowd equals a psychological epidemic I warned you about.

Mean girls are brutal how they shut out & exclude you. It's a peripheral existence/got no friends too.

After her dirty work everyone's contemptuous of you. This was my life after sister abuse [two].

BULLIES AND MISERY

The two sisters would [instantly upon meeting anyone who would listen] give their view on me see.

Next, they hated me for no reason other than the treason they heard from feminist vermin.

Relocation was such sweet rescue from these cobwebs of shrews and their screws. Free, happy, cool.

ESCAPING FEMINISTS/LIBERALS

Feminists are for "restructuring patriarchy" which is the West: tear it down/remake in their image.

Why tear it down? Cuz it's a brutish system predicated on nothing but oppression: that's it man.

Everything is tyranny--capitalism, law and order even--to these feminist types and they are scary.

They all have confirmation bias and thru groupthink they act accordingly and it can be mean see.

Narcissists don't have friends, just a bunch of enablers with the task of spreading his narratives.

GOOD MARRIAGES: AFFINITY

If you have a good marriage you're lucky since it's substitutionary of the original family.

Under a man's protection I could work without interruption nor fear of narcissistic retaliation.

He may not have been neat but he protected me from obstruction/creeps, that's ALL I ever need.

My emotions affected by body like pulling a lever. Stability in the home is a most important buffer.

BULLIES AND MISERY

He protected me/provided stability so I could work full time in sweet privacy with pets surrounding me.

Every ruined relationship was due to drinking. It was a nexus to the devil in me/musta been shocking.

Going baseline wiped out the craving and the addictive personatlity. I became gentle and sweet see.

Up at midnight planning the next day. I expect prosperity: a bright future of invention/felicity.

INHERITED SHAME

Extreme, persistent shame that never goes away is called Inherited Shame: it's not you ok.

It's a big genetic boulder passed down and landing on you--the empath--who meekly takes it on.

With shame going on it's easy for shady characters to take over promising love, riches or whatever.

Some Jezebels say they wanna help, just to get a foot in your door then give everyone the scoop.

The devil comes to steal, kill and destroy and he does it thru Jezebels and wicked men creeping in.

Learn from WWII/how mean people can be. This my dear is the best "head held high" therapy.

Learn what happens to women as evil flows in if they don't have boundaries: it's slavery man.

Happy when alone, with boundaries down your whole life changes into a hell on earth full blown.

People are cruel. You'll be targeted for being good looking or rich. Go solo/ditch the witch.

BULLIES AND MISERY

Your worst enemies are in your own home, the bible says it. Satan divided it so just grow solo.

DESTINY

If you're a woman with purpose & substance put these lessons of human management FIRST sis.

Cuz they'll strip your substance away, smash your depth and even make you ashamed of it.

Where I'm at now, after overcoming all this, is uncanny magic and beauty. There's an end, believe me.

OTHER PEOPLE KEEP US DOWN

What keeps us down/makes us insane? Other people. Study wars and see thru society's charades.

For the people you know? They could change in a minute so stop seeing it as an investment.

God is the One: see the first page of Psalms. The Kings of the earth seek to destroy those of God.

Psalms shows how one man can be a majority with God on his side. Despite 10,000 against him, aye!

The bible describes social psychology perfectly. It's all about dense dullards blocking the heavenly.

REWARDS OF OVERCOMING

To become self-aware, separate from the herd. Then you'll see how absurd they can get dear.

Looking out at my pastures of green with grazing cows but free of human beings I feel so happy/free.

I can appreciate divine beauty in the clouds above, free of narcissistic dramas with crud/duds.

BULLIES AND MISERY

20,000 headshaved women not due to collaboratin' but as a convenient scapegoat at war's end.

Remember that about people. Don't take em so seriously, blaming yourself. Just manage hell.

Manage the people in your life or they'll take control when you let things slide. Head held high!

You learn quickly about people by being in war or a muddle. Solution: live in a bubble/as a couple.

THIS RELATIONSHIP IS DEVASTATING

It puts overload on the body, depletes your resources and to keep surviving whips a dead horse.

His sneaky behavior emptied me of my resources. Before long I was weak and slow of course.

Exhaustion weakens the system running body, for example the metabolic. You gain weight/get sick.

An empath who's had enough recognizes patterns and sees people for who they really are: fluff.

Forgiveness revoked if bad behaviors resurface--since narcs see it as permission for continuance.

Demands are put on your body to maintain survival in a grenade range of change and upheaval.

When exhaustion sets in all systems weaken and the drag means weight gain and depression.

As things grind down diseases set in and now we see how constant stress creates devastation.

Carnivore. Motto: beef, bacon and butter. New kitchen appurtenances: air fryer, grill and smoker.

BULLIES AND MISERY

ALCOHOL AND THE DEVIL

Grandfather said I'd be a great orator or end in the gutter depending on whether I was a drinker.

The last time I drank I went baseline [I died] and came right back, never again craving to imbibe.

HEARTBREAK

WHAT MAKES WOMEN STUPID
FORGET CLOSURE, JUST GET AWAY
AVOID HIS INFLUENCE MISS
A PARASITE DESTROYING THE HOST
DARK EMOTIONS COLOR PERCEPTION
STUCK IN A WAR
IT'S ALWAYS ABOUT CONTROL
JUST GET THE HELL AWAY
FEMALES WHO DON'T FIT
ALL IS COMPENSATORY
THE FEMALE COMMUNITY
OUR REALITY IS EVERYTHING
LET LOWER RUNG [PAST] GO
GIFTS COME BEFORE GREAT MEN
WOMEN FIGHT WITH GOSSIP
I LOVE FASTING/YOU WILL TOO
PULL BANDS TIL IT HURTS
DEMOGRAPHIC CHANGE HURTS

HEARTBREAK

Sudden trauma brings moral collapse and then the world flows in to take advantage/give the axe.

What you're looking at is a snake but you see movie star: a traumatic reversal from past/afar.

WHAT MAKES WOMEN STUPID

We'd be fine alone but humans cast a spell and if unwell from an early hell we cave in that's all.

For every sin there's a compensation in the present moment, it's how our image demotes.

What makes women stupid? They go along with each other not truth with tragic results sis.

After getting the correct narrative they become vehement about it: we've had enough of this!

And as the narrative evolves and changes they go along with that too as if truth is the human zoo.

Women are embarrassingly social thinkers. It's not self generated like a discoverer/ professor.

They get the correct line from TV or friend then act like it's theirs which they'll KILL to defend.

She thinks as her sisters think or to conform to Ms. Social Charm who she wants on her team.

Rise up the ladder and cease being intimidated by mockers on the lower rungs: do it hon'.

HEARTBREAK

They hated you for differences yet you thought it was you, a disgusting fallen princess.

Women brag of independence but then assume the narrative of others: it's pure hypocrisy sister.

It's sickly cyclicity. When people get weak they sink into old cycles instead of growth/success see

FORGET CLOSURE, JUST GET AWAY

Most are not who they say they are or appear to be: the authentic ones are few and far between.

His true self expression is buried after early injuries: the personality is fake/compensatory.

While they are your priority you are just an opportunity: they'll dump you seeing better possibilities.

They are driven into a rage when the external image is dismantled, seeking to kill the culprit.

Things get so bad she gets to the point of running for her life. Escape, exit, never see that guy.

We must learn to separate from anything disagreeing with our well being of which pain is a sign.

The narcissist doesn't operate from a place of divine wisdom. Remember that then trudge on.

The mind must be insulated from the tricks & traps of the narcissist. Is he coming back? No sis.

AVOID HIS INFLUENCE MISS

Curtail conversation. All the small talk and chatter, you don't need that son. Talk basics then run.

HEARTBREAK

"Can't we at least be friends?" That's just bait to hide the hate after you escaped the confusion.

Keep it strictly business. They are incapable of being your friend, that's been proven out sis.

You've gone back a million times in your tired head, now it's time to cut those thoughts instead.

Make no friendship with an angry man and with a furious one do not go. Now, avoid the low.

Avoid this guy lest you learn his ways and get a snare to your soul. That's the pattern you know.

The gross things he says will seep into your speech, his lowness will effect even your dreams.

Control the conversation, as few words as possible and keep it strictly business [give no more info].

NO you can't be friends, he's already proven that. That's a silly trend after all your spats.

He was always two-word Joe but in your head he was a close, intimate connection not a foe.

The hooverer asks too many personal questions, just a way of getting in your heart/head again.

Don't react to toxic encounters from an emotional place, but a spiritual one of evil vs. grace.

In encounters ask holy spirit to lift up a standard against any trick or trap: be armored like a tank.

A PARASITE DESTROYING THE HOST

He's a parasite destroying a host. That's how it should be viewed: no payoff/too high a cost.

HEARTBREAK

There's no payoff but occasional thrills: I pray this won't be your continued love addiction still.

Rest in the arms of Father in heaven while disentrenching from fakes and foes full of leaven.

You were carnal so stuff got by you. But now you're spiritual so it strikes to the core too.

David put space between he and Saul. There was NO CONTACT: it is biblical and spiritual.

A most important exit strategy is denouncing the need for closure--ain't gonna get it with a loser.

David just accepted Saul: no need to know "why" he wanted to kill him, it's irrelevant that's all.

Never get hung up on "why" just save your life and avoid that guy. Even he doesn't know why, aye.

It's like tinted glass was put over a bright happy life. It affected every perception, all was strife.

All you saw was first filtered thru "him". He was an APP driving perception, your operating system.

You wanna get your own blissful and happy reality back, uncolored by that manipulator and hack.

It's like a giant boulder called "hate" which suddenly disperses to God's love when he's gone ok.

DARK EMOTIONS COLOR PERCEPTION

All perception is colored by the same dark emotion. Making gold is transmutation then elation.

Closure is the idea I need something to be spoken or done to accept reality, like an apology.

HEARTBREAK

Closure is a search for WHY. It's a turgid merry go around in the mind: give it up and FLY.

Asking for closure is a subconscious hope of remaining possibilities. Can I get him back maybe?

Once hot turns cold there's no way he'll change back again except maybe--if you're finally gone.

Whether you did something to turn off the tap is irrelevant in fact, just get out FAST.

EXIT and cheat the hangman. Cuz it's gonna get rough in you stay in that matrix, believe it man.

There's no more possibilities and you thinking there may be is degrading: cut him loose, be a lady.

Be like Lucas McCain [the Rifleman]: disdain evil and show it, teach your kids it, avoid bedlam.

People are so cruel it sickens you. That shows you're still in the stew: look forward to happy Sue.

You've been in a war with a narcissist, a self-involved strategist aiming to conquer then dismiss.

STUCK IN A WAR

I stayed stuck in a war I blamed them for. I could never see it was ME trusting treachery.

You are here, they are there. It will never happen again, it's just morbid history for the trash bind.

You stayed stuck in the ringer sucking all the life and spirit outa you: from Elite to a beginner.

He calls for a bootie call, he creeps back into your house and you think all will now be well.

HEARTBREAK

Evil men like him are a loose canon. You can expect anything and you won't be ready, Karen.

Any bad habit is addiction = SIN. It obstructs all you do, is always in the way, makes em hate you too.

IT'S ALWAYS ABOUT CONTROL

Humans seek to control and influence others. This is so dangerous, teach this to sons/daughters.

They give you a gift, they're seeking to influence so you easily assume their dangerous narrative.

Lucas was vigilant about what's said in the home in front of Mark. Out you go if words are dark.

Closure is a hidden hope of remaining possibilities. Don't do lunch or dinner over it surely.

Mind Myths: Closure will lead to repentance and he'll fall on his knees asking for forgiveness.

The idea of closure perpetuates the connection between you and toxicity: give it up honey.

The need for closure keeps the wound open and indicates you're still sick and beggin'.

JUST GET THE HELL AWAY

Get the hell away for he's dangerous, ok? The closure neuroses is from media and a false fix.

He's a blistering boiling hot stove to you Sue and you still can't see it, pursuing like a fool.

Get the hell away for he's dangerous. Closure neuroses will destroy and is a false fix.

HEARTBREAK

He'll never be for you/always be jealous, constitutionally incapable of getting beyond this.

Having been prey I'm concerned for your welfare. I pray for right decisions: to stop going there.

I know the gut ache from love/rejection, I've well aware of this predicament/predilection.

When mature don't look back to when obedient to a derelict or lunatic. Block it out: sick.

FEMALES WHO DON'T FIT

Females who don't fit are called Inconvenient Women, burned as witches from the beginning.

People get mentally ill just as they do physically ill and it'd be temporary if no [SRIs] meds see.

I fuel the tank at dawn, I pull the bands later on, I enjoy the view as perception reveals ALL.

God knew that them putting me down would fire ambition in me like you've never known.

When the hedge is down it's like going into the underworld or visiting hell: build a wall.

Her relatives considered her worthless, shirking all gainful employment to work on her thesis.

ALL IS COMPENSATORY

"All is compensatory" is a saying in psychology. Sin brings compensation-- that's its sign see.

I'm a worker, I start at midnight. I find it fascinating assembling a puzzle that God predesigned.

HEARTBREAK

Women brag of independence but then assume the narrative of others: it's pure hypocrisy sister.

While working and waiting for success you may be on the fringes of society: just have patience.

The genotype potential in man is genius as he brings through theories of great importance.

One looks back terrified of what coulda happened. Getting clear we're more aware of the bad.

You can see right through people now. No second guessing, you're an expert on mobs.

Separate what they say from the truth. Now send the gossip to the bin and be proud of you.

THE FEMALE COMMUNITY

The female community evolves the topics and they get more and more vehement about it.

The more mutual agreement exists the more they tend to get really pissed, causing us stress.

They read some new book and it becomes a fad or trend then we're supposed to adapt to them?

They too are a flash in the pan but not doing anything. Don't wait to die: pursue your destiny.

We swam in muddy waters and literally didn't know any better. That's how to view the others.

God bless women, who men have erased. Thru history ignored/scorned, defiled and displaced.

A person or nation without faith is always searching for identity. Its sad to see: danger/treachery.

HEARTBREAK

You're living in a past era that doesn't even exist: They died/moved on/couldn't care less.

Go back to the past, there's no one there. It never works to relapse, no one even cares.

OUR REALITY IS EVERYTHING

Our reality is everything. Keep it present, look ahead, be like Paul who focused on forgetting.

Don't know why God chose me to be a vessel for a Creative Act so wonderful/I'm special.

The censorship on facebook is preposterous--self-evident truths are banned by nuts.

Don't waste the time you have left resurrecting the past. It was just a lesson but long passed.

The lower rungs were pure hell hon', being mocked, belittled and scorned--but it's GONE.

It's hard dealing with affluent relatives on the wrong page, a camel thru a needle is easier ok.

I was banned for saying Nazi Germany stressed the collective over the individual--crazy.

LET LOWER RUNG [PAST] GO

The lower rung lessons were hellish, being invaded by inferiors, mocked and belittled as trash.

Your time is limited so look ahead and create instead. Lessons have good effects but are dead.

Homeless on trashy cold streets or living in gated places with billionaire elites? Set your sights!

HEARTBREAK

Your time is limited, why shouldn't you go to the top and really live it: the good life, so go for it.

Set your sights on Palm Beach or Santa Barbara, envision a life of creative power in America.

To get privacy I bought the whole street. No one there but that's ok, it's quiet solitude I need.

GIFTS COME BEFORE GREAT MEN

Your gifts will bring you before great men. They'll be very impressed as your groove begins.

Ok so you failed before. Let's try it again for you're so much better: prepared/not looking poor.

Hedges for privacy, verandas for views. Charming nooks in the home and fine aromas too.

Democrats do the globalist's bidding by bashing our country tho' they say it's the hippies.

When I went wrong it was across the board. As a consequence many memories gush forth.

Note to women: you must be financially independent lest you're forced to do what you shouldn't.

Her desire for identity was super strong to discount and override her mother/sister put downs.

One may say it was strong enough to build a battleship for that's what life was: war and torment.

I'm finally ready for the best talents ripen late. It's all about triggering recognition in them ok.

Shame memories are peculiar to you and lock in your muscles and GSR [galvanic skin response].

HEARTBREAK

If memories are socially based when you repent [a major change] they are all negated/erased.

That's the Good News. With our repentance the slate's wiped clean and we get a new chance.

People are intrusive, invasive and officious. They'll spread it all around the block kids.

WOMEN FIGHT WITH GOSSIP

Gossip/sly slander is their armory. Think of that, how dangerous it is while looking innocent see.

You got a problem talk to me about it. Don't go behind my back, wreck my rep and incite riots.

Social females are on the horn all day managing people and then ostracizing the disagreeable.

The gossip weapon is viscous, cruel, calculating and can get you killed as it builds and builds.

After relocating to a safe sane place it still took three years to recalibrate [reset to normalcy] ok.

You only get one chance and then you're dead. Don't bank on your reincarnation, this is it.

A desire to be remembered after death is a rational one so we leave the earth what benefits them.

Did they hate you for sins or because you weren't part of them [for they cover for their own]?

I LOVE FASTING/YOU WILL TOO

When you get to the point when even water causes acid and burping it's time to stop eating.

HEARTBREAK

Just one piece of cheese and orthorexia was gone and a panorama replaced fruitarian tunnel vision.

She was so depleted/sick of being cheated her skin just hung on her, her psychology reversed.

Eat at dawn, exercise in afternoon. Fasting with exercise evokes HGH: human growth hormone.

PULL BANDS TIL IT HURTS

Pull those bands, the muscles tend to atrophy and the skin shrivels up too see. Pull: 1 - 2 - 3...

Deathbed: If the grapes don't work we switch to Jagermeister to cross the great river.

When you eat have the most calorically dense food you can find. Levoy Finicum, Cane Beds

Eat the calorically dense for satiety power and let THAT determine food values--it's for survival.

A salad/smoothie and you're soon hungry again. That's not smart/we gotta readjust friends.

Succulent produce is great with a meal but to rely totally on it is inefficient with no SP: Satiety Power.

Add fat so you won't have to eat again. How about melted butter on your donut friend.

To look good--AMAZING--you need enough calories for that sugar punch at dawn. Now fast on.

I want eating to be in back of me all day. Not in front, always thinking about it inefficiently.

I want glorious fastarian consciousness all day, never thinking of food taking 85% of our energy.

HEARTBREAK

85% of our energy goes to digestion, assimilation and elimination. To release this, just imagine!

I want that creative energy UP in my head, all day. That is the happiest space folks, try it ok.

DEMOGRAPHIC CHANGE HURTS

Demographic change [mass replacement] hurts like hell as your piece of the pie dwindles to nil.

If we're not safe we're not sovereign, period. If a sense of security is trashed we're powerless.

Not everyone is born in a safe place. You'll have to relocate once you see facts/seek safety.

It's difficult to get a man to understand something when his salary depends on him not getting it.

End slavery: get a gun. Constitution allows self defense against lunatic mobs/government.

Communism et. al. are atheistic ideologies threatened by God and the family, even history.

Globalists thru the hippies sought to destroy America since the sixties. This is the endgame see.

Democrats do the globalist's bidding by crashing America tho' they think it's the hippies.

Hippies/liberal women think it's their own thinkin' but it's all about thoughts socially driven.

"This is what I think" they say then spill out the same narrative drummed in from early days.

They'll go to any lengths to prove it right and ruin their lives cuz it's out of grace/based on strife.

AFFINITY OR MISERY

CRUEL ON THE WAY DOWN
LITTLE **GIRL** POLITIX
PEOPLE LOVE TO HATE
PEACE VS. THE HARD HEART
IT'S THEIR CRAP NOT YOURS
TWO SAVING DEVICES
RE-SEE IT ALL IN MIND
NARCISSISM IS DEFENSE MECHANISM
IMMATURE AND SENSUAL
THE HERD IS A COMPLEX COBWEB
SHAME IS DUMPED
FOCUS ON YOUR GOOD POINTS
ESSENTIAL SOLITUDE FOR THE SENSITIVE
A MONSTROUS TASK: FORGIVING THE PAST
SIGNS OF TOXIC SIBLINGS
THE DIVA SYNDROME
SIGNS OF HUMAN WEAKNESS
SERIAL BULLIES IN THE FAMILY
COMPELLED TO CAUSE TROUBLE
THEY SCREAM AND BARK
ALIENATION FROM YOUR PACK
MEAN LIBERAL ROBOTS & PUPPETS
GLOBALISM IS LOST IDENTITY AND FEELINGS
IF NOT TAUGHT BOUNDARIES, BAD LUCK
PTSD: INTRUSIVE MEMORIES
SHE BARKED AT ME
HIX POLITIX
DIVERSITY MEANS WHITE REPLACEMENT
THEY HAVE NO RIGHT TO BE HERE
AS THE THIRD WORLD CLEANS OUT
THE BORDER IS EVERYTHING
WHEN THEY'RE NOT CHOPPING OFF HEADS
CUBA/CALIFORNIA IS WARM/BEAUTIFUL
AMERICANS WANT THE BORDER SECURED!

AFFINITY OR MISERY

MOON AND THE BRUTISH CARNAL MAN
TRUMPISM EXPLODING ACROSS THE WORLD
TRUMP IS BREAKING HOAXES LIKE TPP
MULTICULTURALISM IS PERVERSION/COMMUNISM
GOD KNOWS NO COWARDS
SOCIALISM IS *ELITE* IN CONTROL NOT YOU
NATIONALISM IS PROPER AND NORMAL
TRUMPISM IS SPREADING QUICKLY
QUISLING TRAITORS MUST GO
KEEP CHAOS TO BRING EM IN
DESTRUCTIVE OBSESSION WITH RACE: DIVERSITY
MASS MIGRATION TO LEVEL THE NATION
ULTRA-RICH LOVE COLLECTIVISM
FRENCH NOT CAPTURED ANYMORE!
DEMOCRATS USE ACTORS/COMEDIANS
GLOBALISTS USE PSYCH WARFARE
ELITES WANT US MAD AT COPS
MUSLIMS HATE DOGS LET ALONE CATS
DON'T TELL ME WE'RE THE SAME
THERE IS NO WAR ON WOMEN (IN THE WEST)
WHEN DOES ALTRUISM BECOME ROBBERY?
MULTICULTURALISM SINCE THE SIXTIES
LEFTIST UNIVERSITIES HATE AMERICA
THE RUSSIAGATE SCAM
LIBERALISM USED TO MEAN HUMANE
THE NEW RENAISSANCE IF HE'S BACK IN
RATIONALIZATION DRIVES CULTURE WAR
GOAL OF NOW: TEN REGIONS/NO NATIONS
KEEP SMALL TOWNS INTACT
THE CHIC WILL BE UP A CREEK
THE DUMB PUT THE SMART DOWN
WELLNESS UPDATES
WHAT AM I SUPPOSED TO EAT

AFFINITY OR MISERY

CRUEL ON THE WAY DOWN

The older I get the more evil I realize they were. As denial lifts I'm sickened but God is here.

When I woke up to the game, the matrix, the system I was a new person: the cure is education.

When I met her she sized me up, looked me up and down and hated my guts like an obdurate dog.

The jealous sibling tells lies about victim to the parents. Happy childhood ends this hurts so much.

A shameless brutal psychopath you keep forgiving thinking now you'll be so happy with him.

Like a camp survivor I finally got the right perspective and been happily secluded ever since.

Don't take my precious daily freedom away and when you come unannounced you do that ok.

All narcissists treat other people as objects but without empathy the relationship turns sadistic.

LITTLE GIRL POLITIX

Forgive em for they know not what they do--fine, I'll do that but only after finally going no-contact.

Pain is great, it registers deep and body keeps score--diseases/lost sleep--but you're unaware see.

AFFINITY OR MISERY

The trauma of being devalued, falsely compared, jilted, rejected by someone you respect, heck!

Don't worry they're always too into their own thing to remember yours except to blame of course.

People are cruel so you gotta be in control at all times. That means self-control lest again evil rise.

From the foregoing you now know the rules of the game. Now when the bully gets uppity you gain.

She can't escape into the arms of a man anymore or be his dam whore just to avoid the bully girl.

That's what women do: they aren't nymphomaniacs they just want protection/I've been there too.

PEOPLE LOVE TO HATE

I wanted someone to know I existed, to pay a little attention, to not hit or gossip about me.

You never did and you still don't so that's how I know. If they aren't on your life level, exit and go.

It's almost like people love to hate. They wouldn't know what to think if they didn't get so irate.

Your body keeps score, so after a long trauma you're like to be exhausted tho' you don't know it.

Even if it happened years back and the culprits are dead in fact you still gotta recuperate ol' chap.

It was cruel but they're dead. It was reprehensible but they're in a rest home/can't even remember it.

Disagree and they'll take your money/ruin your life: the loving liberal totalitarians like Trudeau, aye.

AFFINITY OR MISERY

Why do they all hate that woman? She makes mistakes like everyone--so what if she has passion.

The minute the weak get an edge up they take over every time. Recall the Jezebel in power, aye.

Just the fact you were a pin cushion meant you hadn't learned your lesson so now forget it hon'

If you're gonna be a smart ass first you gotta be smart otherwise you're just an ass. J. Kennedy

PEACE VS. THE HARD HEART

God said He already gave peace to us but we upset that. Rely on that, relax, know God wants it.

Only the pure in heart can see God. That means watch anger, nip those divisive emotions in the bud.

Without self-protection [clarity] one's heart gets hard and that's the one thing blocking God.

Forgiveness is so crucial in saving ourselves it helps torealize that hurting people hurt people always.

Forgiveness is so crucial to us it really helps to realize that hurting people hurt people always.

Once we start to complain it's all we see. The opposite is remaining thankful for all God's bounty.

Since ingratitude and bitterness is the great obstruction to God's goodness, ask Him to help with this.

So you got robbed. God'll put holes in their bucket and double you each moment as promised.

IT'S THEIR CRAP NOT YOURS

AFFINITY OR MISERY

They wanna project their crap onto you so you feel like crap but it's someone else's--not your map.

Instead of being unequally yoked to people be yoked to Jesus by casting your care, a life share.

I ask Him to share my jealousies or anything else holding me back from my destiny see.

Since we're yoked together He doesn't want me putting myself down either. It's a two way winner.

One of the greatest helps for PTSD is finding the silver lining to everything--like I always had beauty.

Filled with bitterness I couldn't see God's goodness. You can be pitiful or powerful, not both.

Heal to empower those rising above oppression their family had over them--that hellish bedlam.

How could a family produce such darkness? It's a mess, the cobweb illusions of the envious.

Toxic siblings can't steal the shining inner light within you but it goes opaque when confused.

TWO SAVING DEVICES

These two devices worked magic instantly. Find silver lining/see the positive and share with Jesus.

Here I saw my entire life as a series of wars now I saw I always lived in a mansion as a discoverer.

I always had my herb, always had my music and a beautiful view. Thoughts were deep too.

Decide to see the past positively. I always stayed in beautiful homes learning about treachery.

AFFINITY OR MISERY

Instead of peeved thoughts over. abuse, think: I had all my bills paid, I lived in a beautiful house.

RE-SEE IT ALL IN MIND

Whatever it is, re-see it in mind. Then I saw I had always lived in beauty of the extraordinary kind.

Amidst all the abuse and treachery and drinking and arguments, there was beauty all around!

The other key for me was whenever I was feeling bad, share it with Jesus as if yoked together.

It's called State Dependent Memory: what we recall's dependent on the mental state we're in!

Could I be wrong about all these thoughts and recalls I've been having? It's a sliding variable truly.

Positive: while I was acting out all my demons God always had me in a mansion. Just imagine.

While I was being hurt, minimized and rejected I had a beautiful view, magnificent and majestic.

NARCISSISM IS DEFENSE MECHANISM

Narcissism is a defense mechanism, it's a coping strategy and it's from terrible trauma usually.

When your friends love you on your way down but in your winning season they're not around.

Can they celebrate you? That's the test when you approach your apex--are they still jealous?

These people are freaks. The word dishonesty applies to all of them: Ted Nugent on liberals.

AFFINITY OR MISERY

I was blessed with high perception and it's caused nothing but trouble with the rabble.

Reading between the lines or seeing hidden truths is regarded as paranoid/needing drugs too.

Evil exists on the earth and if you're weak it's like a magnet to maggots then you're cursed.

IMMATURE AND SENSUAL

These people are immature, sensual, undisciplined, craven, brazen, grabby selfish demons.

Being compassionate with yourself is the most important thing to do after enduring this.

I never realized what immaturity looked like 'til I met those boys. I was beyond sickened/amazed.

It hurts looking back but we're compelled to do so. Try looking ahead instead to high life not low.

You get married innocently then suddenly you're the evil stepmother, a projection and archetype.

Then suddenly you're in competition with stepchildren and it affects your looks and their derision.

THE HERD IS A COMPLEX COBWEB

Welcome to the human herd, a complex cobweb that can ruin your entire life by a social curse.

Being different but not knowing enough to sequester I was a battering ram for any man I let in.

There's no house big enough for two women: That's the saying of truth about female competition.

AFFINITY OR MISERY

Being held down, manipulated, gaslighted & smeared is a life lesson about which there's no forgettin'

Being held hostage in your home as grifters move in on you is a life lesson: now we're finally alone.

Number One: Try to let go of your biggest unhealthy emotion, SHAME. I felt it all the time ok.

SHAME IS DUMPED

When nastiness/disdain is dumped on you for years it's not that easy to wash it off with tears.

I cried like a little girl--that's how far I'd fallen with their rejection, to better look "up to" them.

Tho' we're imperfect human beings we ALL have wonderful traits/qualities-- focus on these.

The Jezebel imposed on me just by opening her big mouth and lurching for her many wants.

She intruded on and triangulated every conversation. Her social invasions caused aggravation.

You can't trust her. She'll ruin your marriage and hit on your husband sure as I'm standing here.

Save your life and get away from Jezebel. She sends family, neighborhoods, churches to hell.

FOCUS ON YOUR GOOD POINTS

We must focus on the good now. What's loving, uplifting, motivating and finally, hope giving.

Kindness, what brings us joy and peace--this changes our lives as we leave hell without cease.

AFFINITY OR MISERY

This will change your conscious reality sis and when you think about it that's all there is.

Victimized, traumatized and feeling like we are never enough. Then settling for less/the rough.

ESSENTIAL SOLITUDE FOR THE SENSITIVE

Highly sensitive people must carve out time alone, otherwise they're always in reaction and dull.

The dysfunctional family has a lack of empathy. You wish to converse but they're toxic see.

They will never empathize nor understand you. Only misunderstandings await if you pursue.

We want them to understand so it hurts but if we persist it's over: must see the Dunning Kruger.

Dunning Kruger: As the dumb take over the sensitives are pushed aside as supremacists or whatever.

It's scary as dumb take over cuz they'll never understand the clever so down goes culture.

It's scary cuz you know you can't make em understand. You can only pray they'll go easy man.

See The Pianist. You get what they give or less. Life's a bitch so be grateful for what you have sis.

Gratitude is the key unlocking God's power to give you more. Ingrates are hated by all/stop it now.

I cried so I looked weak and that confirmed the bad rap from that creep but it's God I will seek.

The parents spill the beans without saying who said it see, increasing the dysfunctional scene.

AFFINITY OR MISERY

The wonderful things about you the black sheep: Self growth, spiritual growth and final victory.

You have gifts/strengths & it's your life purpose to follow that—what you're meant to be, got it?

A MONSTROUS TASK: FORGIVING THE PAST

It's easier to forget abusers if seeing people as archetypes/life levels you had to learn about.

You had little schemers and users in your life cuz you were unbelievably naive in that area, aye.

Sibling abuse isn't a one shot deal. It's a million incidents by the cruel until you finally heal.

Forgive, purify heart, resume perfect step with God. Don't forgive, stay dark, miss the mark.

Forgive, release and TRANSCEND these people for they're merely little while you're regal.

People aren't perfect, they're born lost and filthy sinners so how do they treat little sisters?

Rise above the jealous nobodies you've known who held you down/trashed your rep in town.

Repent then don't think about gremlins who were your education about the evil nature of humans.

Test of a knight: can he forgive those slights? Or is the ego still in control and just wants to fight?

SIGNS OF TOXIC SIBLINGS

It's all about dysfunction, narcissism and unhealthy relationships. What are these signs?

AFFINITY OR MISERY

Discredit you, distort the truth about you, twist every word you say and repeat evil rumors ok.

What's the cure for frustration? Stop the silence and start telling your stories sisters/brethren.

They gotta hate someone so it's gonna be you since you're there and they wanna have some fun.

It makes it far more difficult dealing with Christian toxic siblings--something to think about see.

A toxic sibling won't cheer you on/be happy for success nor ever applaud your achievements.

Everyone is to some extent a narcissist, it's a question of harm but most importantly, empathy.

In an effort to fend off that hurt the child creates the false self which is everything he is not.

So the false self is omnipotent, knows everything, is only in him, it's his one and only salvation.

Above all, the false self is invulnerable and impermeable--he's not gonna let you in girl.

THE DIVA SYNDROME

Liberal feminists suck--they're underhanded. Don't let em in cuz they'll want everything you have.

Let's call it the Diva Syndrome: She wants it all to herself balancing factions all day long.

She wants what you have and deviously will work towards that including your dear husband, dog or cat.

I was able to explain and overcome it but Don wasn't--he died in the desert in a lonely trailer, dam her.

AFFINITY OR MISERY

"I took a course and I'm compassionate, forgiving, kind" yet still a jealous bitch, never you mind.

SIGNS OF HUMAN WEAKNESS

Disgusting beta males look at wife's face before speaking. I can't tell you how this irks me.

She's so "compassionate and kind" but disfriended me--a family member--for being excellent.

I'm not gonna insult/debase my keen intelligence by going to your puerile page again your Highness.

It's all true but you're not addressing the main problem: them and even the churches are dumbed down.

I think of the MILLIONS of pets killed by angry kids to get back at mom who dared to lay boundaries.

The PTSD gets worse when older cuz you're more mature, in the original events you see the danger.

Stop wasting time on that guy and get back to work. This obsession is gone so drop the curse.

Living in the desert wilderness for 30 years preserved me from conflict and signs of aging disappeared.

I had long bouts of solitude even years. But when "they" came it was DISASTER and I needed repair.

SERIAL BULLIES IN THE FAMILY

That dissipated old lady in a rest home was a serial bully who ruined countless lives sweetie.

The only times I showed signs of aging was when you came around cuz it was so unbearably long.

AFFINITY OR MISERY

In the Diva Syndrome she controls every dam thing including who meets who in your own family.

When I meet the jealous female I feel sick to my stomach, lost, degraded, abandoned, hated.

After being with you I just want my cats and stop talking about that, they're precious/you're not.

She was a jealous hyper-controlling bitch calling herself a loving helpful friend but NEVER AGAIN.

I can't go back cuz I grew too much separating FROM. I'm in a whole new world my own free of dumb.

I'm so prolific now that I'm married and relocated, that is: protected and secure, happy and square.

COMPELLED TO CAUSE TROUBLE

You could never hope to compete so just shut up. But you can't, can you—you gotta cause trouble.

I'm in my own universe flying high above the herd. It feels so good leaving you behind for a new world.

California's ready to de-criminalize, decarcerate and de-police all the while murders rapidly increase.

FAKING: It's the in-thing to be non-white and the world hates white people so this is totally predictable.

Neurotic styles like the Diva Syndrome vanish with death, they're just clusters of energy in this life.

Think of the pets. They don't want the TV on they want MUSICA! If you make them happy it's God.

The lovey dovey huggy thing is just a compensation with women as a member of the club of vermin.

AFFINITY OR MISERY

Yes women may be oversensitive to words but those words bely an evil heart revealing worlds.

THEY SCREAM AND BARK

She **SCREAMED** and **BARKED** at me then later apologized but I just couldn't see her again, really terrified.

After the friggin' maid called me old I got rid of her instantly but later noticed she also stole.

Don't dare get into the car with a woman driver she'll intentionally make your life miserable sir.

She'll take you where you don't wanna go like all her own errands thinking nothing of you in the car.

What a realization of **COMPLETION**: The work has all been done just sit back and enjoy the ride son.

I'm sorry I just don't like your choice of music so I'll stay away cuz I like my own world better ok.

It's the realization I don't have to do anything/the work has already been done that's so much fun.

After completion don't look at the data. You're not of this world anymore/all that stuff you're above now.

You had your baby, you completed the Creative Act put in you before your birth [fact] so now just relax.

Whether it "sells" or doesn't sell is not up to me, I've given it to the world and now I'm just gonna be.

What is the result of separation from the pack? SHAME. That's why you feel it/you're not to blame.

The family were a buncha liberals who didn't know what they were talking about and threw you out.

AFFINITY OR MISERY

ALIENATION FROM YOUR PACK

You felt alienated from the pack, SCARED in fact. That's how it feels to be so different, a real sad sack.

The terrifying gut feeling being different from the pack only subsided by getting solitude way out.

I was horrified, terrified and sickened when I first entered Kindergarten facing peers of my generation.

I was so terrified of the liberals my gut ached and then an eating disorder. Food ya' know means mother.

I was horrified, terrified, sickened by my family members. It hurts to say this about sisters or brothers.

It wasn't until midlife I realized all these people problems were from LIBERALS causing all the strife.

I was conservative at 12 after reading a Taylor Caldwell novel but others were far left mindless liberal.

But it was after my two older sisters came back from liberal colleges that it all broke loose.

Their ideas were horrible, disruptive, depressing along with blaming accusations like privilege.

They were angry & snooty about it as if we were intellectually inferior dumbs compared to them.

MEAN LIBERAL ROBOTS & PUPPETS

If emergency is enough to take our freedoms pretty soon we have constant crises/no freedoms

Trudeau's not worried about people spreading a virus it's their obstinance refusing his rule he resists.

AFFINITY OR MISERY

They're not big thinkers, they're pure party line. Trudeau and several others globally primed.

Every neoliberal robot with power came thru globalist priming: carbon copies without brains.

These sleek little robots are backed by big money and they believe in centralized gov and tyranny.

When you invoke the holocaust you diminish the great catastrophic human tragedy that it was.

Justin accuses of swastikas when no one's been more Hitlerian in his dictator-like takeover.

When cities burned to the ground by BLM Trump was called a tyrannical fascist/Justin loved this.

But when Justin is honked out he declares Martial Law and destroys their bank accounts/jobs.

GLOBALISM IS LOST IDENTITY AND FEELINGS

Then my globalist sister married a Hindu and he took over our Christian family. Talk about catastrophe.

Not saying wrong or right but what do they have in common really? Mom left Christianity.

How he treated animals in the labs for example--America was a decent country and I was miserable.

If you keep falling for his line over and over, at a certain point you're no longer a victim but a volunteer.

There's nothing to do that hasn't been done or said. So lets just go on and wait for what God has.

You will HAVE nothing, you will OWN nothing and you will LOVE IT! Liberal Advertisement

AFFINITY OR MISERY

Genetic potential for weird mental illness is there but only extreme stress triggers the symptoms flare.

Not a nickel to the evil liberals when it comes time to decide the will. You can't support hell.

You have genetic potentials for talents but also mental illnesses. It can go either way so be careful sis.

Big modern churches: fake corporate "positive" and glitzy Satanic energy, seductive and unreal.

They were horrible, I had no idea. The schools created little criminals and I'm worried about your pets.

PTSD made me victim since in memory a tiny woman can't stand up to gang of boys in their twenties.

I felt overwhelmed with vulnerability even though they were now in prison, a sense of little ol' me.

We can't feel vulnerable due to small size, women would stay ultra-fat otherwise, as is described.

You wield power in such a way you don't have to be big to do it. Like Big Valley/Barbara Stanwick

I was a weakling--no power--cuz I ever let em anywhere near me in the first place: I faced this.

I probably needed their approval or thought I could change them! No more of this ma'am.

IF NOT TAUGHT BOUNDARIES, BAD LUCK

If a child isn't taught boundaries he'll learn it later thru invasion/evil cuz unless you're fenced it's over.

How to decrease extreme sense of vulnerability: raise your boundaries. A weak woman's out to please.

AFFINITY OR MISERY

You please your husband, kids, pets or whoever you want but NEVER give into demands from nuts.

The end of strife: He said one word and I never wanna see the creep again for the rest of my life.

They treated you that way cuz you were crazy and addicted but it wasn't them/it's predicted.

God kept you in the mess just long enough to learn the lesson then wrenched you free, home again.

I may look normal like everything's all right but inside my head is intrusive memories day and night.

Don't fear when God saved you just in time. He revealed the awful foe but was there just the same.

Had you been strong like you are today it never would've happened. Rid remorse by recalling that.

Allowing myself to be insulted by you is like walking into a dark dungeon and I'll never do it again.

PTSD: INTRUSIVE MEMORIES

I wanna be clear, totally here in the present. Not cluttered with past events I can't do a thing about.

It's a dirty contaminated mind filled with past crap that'll disperse/be non-ap the minute we pass.

I wanna be free of what you did to me so I can love again without projections and transferences see.

Intrusive Memories are the characteristic of PTSD you see, they popup when you're never ready.

It's extremely inefficient to have memories popup at worst times, blocking our creative action sublime.

AFFINITY OR MISERY

To be Christian soldiers we must be pliable as God's spirit comes through, not all blocked up in a stew.

I suppose the intrusive memories are there so I can finish up here but I look forward to being clear.

I don't wanna live in the past I wanna chop off the past only retaining the lessons therein, at last.

You assumed I was just like you, well I'm not. You were presumptuous there and I instantly got out.

Anyone who's been thru their own personal war like I have won't put up with degradation anymore.

Ask any woman: how many times you been battled down by other women in a mean tirade of aggression?

SHE BARKED AT ME

She opened up her big mouth and BARKED at me. I'm still shaking just recalling it--is this just me?

I'm not gonna compete with mediocre stuff you're into. I've withdrawn back into my home/in SITU.

A 53 year old feminist hit me once cuz we disagreed. Violence is happening in female pugnacity.

Modern women think they have a right to be continually FURIOUS in fact that's their favorite word.

At the other end are the polygamous wives instructed to "keep sweet" no matter what, I prefer that.

If you're novel, new, fresh, unique, different they freak out. They don't know how to think, no doubt.

The bully uppity mean girls will dissociate from you at the grocery store with their nose up in the air.

AFFINITY OR MISERY

I hate their despicable guts and the female community is the biggest obstruction to female genius.

A million selfies but what about solid work? Something substantial, what have you done jerk?

Being invaded by gang of boys coulda been God's plan because I learned a library of books from it.

The evil helper offered to drive me someplace and put me thru misery for hours--this is commonplace.

HIX POLITIX

Votes and cheap labor, period: that's why they let em in and it's serious.

Two immigration concerns: Going on the dole and refusing to join the whole.

If you reward illegals with amnesty there will be more of them and more fraud and that's against God

Not one democrat's against illegal immigration today: need a fast track to citizenship says Hillary.

For Austria a border isn't enough they also sent troops to defend it--Europe is finally getting tough.

EU punishes countries refusing to be flooded with migrants like Germany.

DIVERSITY MEANS WHITE REPLACEMENT, PERIOD

Diversity means: non-whites replacing whites, genocide.

Obviously we can't let people into our country unvetted but the liberals want all borders invaded.

They're barbaric but you don't believe it. You'd rather have approval--admit it. Denial: repent of it.

Opposing illegal immigration is "racist". This is the reality we must swallow whole from the fascists.

AFFINITY OR MISERY

They don't call it "communism" but "globalism"--all bought by the same interests: corporate fascism.

Globalism is anti-family: seeks to break everyone up. Divorce is no more a stigma but a feather in their cap.

For the sake of our pets, fix our borders. America was decent as we love our pets as sons/daughters.

Suddenly we're surrounded by strangers--a tsunami of God's wrath as our land is filled with dangers.

We sense we're in a clamping cage where a diabolical plan (huge) is closing despite our rage.

The left's sympathy for immigrants seems peculiar vs. apathy for small town America and it's future.

The left wants open borders--that's "sympathy" as the Southwest goes into chaos and disorder.

A population bomb's as devastating to America as a suitcase nuke. That's gonna sink the ship dude

Obama violated constitution and thus Trump ended DACA program.

THEY HAVE NO RIGHT TO BE HERE

They don't have a right to be here to begin with--it was an illegal order by the ill-legit so shut up twit.

Gang-tattooed dreamers in their forties.

Europeans want borders so Hungary walled off Serbia, Macedonia/Greece and Slovenia/Croatia.

Any death occurring during commission of a felony is homicide.

A nation has the right to secure it's borders: to know who's coming and who they are--we've fallen so far.

AFFINITY OR MISERY

Illegals unschooled in constitutional guarantees and individual liberties: workers for huge leftist cities.

How globalist totalitarianism works: put people in head positions from fascist countries ruled by clerks.

God's wrath comes through disasters or relocation of large groups: suddenly surrounded by strangers.

How the criminals fell the mighties: foreign-borns in high positions from anti-democratic fascist societies.

The lawlessness of Mexico is being allowed to implode into the U.S. They're pouring in and catered to (fuss).

The new voting block (immigrant children) are fed far better than our children in the schools. Fools.

AS THE THIRD WORLD CLEANS OUT

As the Third World cleans out there is tens of millions more a month--are you ready to be debunked?

The militia's been called to scout the Texan border and stem the tide against gangs or disorder--when?

The borders are overrun by disease and gangs. They're wide open but no one cares about such things.

We have open borders and Fox won't report it. Terrorists/gangs are getting through but we must stand it.

What's the worst misery of all? Ruled by foreign troops. That's the scoop and it applies to all groups.

Terrorists coming across and they don't care--they'd rather be politically correct: a cultural scare.

Not letting them in, he was shipping them in. A steady stream of future democrats to our chagrin.

AFFINITY OR MISERY

THE BORDER IS EVERYTHING

The border fight is bringing all to light. Out of bad comes good? Out of sight--I'm encouraged tonite.

To the left (enraged mourners): A better way forward is to reflect, absorb, gather strength/constructively oppose.

Cuba's warm and beautiful but we gotta look past the climate: It's about evil leadership, believe it.

Bad guys are the only ones who can have guns in France. Aren't liberal socialists dumb-asses?

Think of this, in the greatest country on earth: a communist is the contender--how absurd!

Hillary's wearing communist MAO outfits from the era when he was killing millions of party misfits.

Relativism is killing us. Being told all religions are the same and if we don't like the flood, we're racists.

WHEN THEY'RE NOT CHOPPING OFF HEADS

If they're not chopping off heads they believe in those who do or Shariah law and it's the opposite to us.

The pope along with Obama wants to destroy our way of life. This is not about love/goodness, only strife.

The public schools are "progressive" (communist): Everything that is yours is mine too, honest.

CUBA/CALIFORNIA IS WARM/BEAUTIFUL

Cuba/Calfiornia is warm and beautiful too but we must look at political tyranny as the wider issue.

The well-organized money movers think beyond nation-states and empower their un-elected classmates.

AFFINITY OR MISERY

All the rest are poll-iticians easily bought by offshore banksters exempt from these laws, as we rot.

Big bucks are being spent to bring Trump down--threatened by this anti-globalist who isn't a con.

Do you think this pope is a man of God just cuz a bunch of men said he was? Look past images/applause.

Being a "socialist" means you hate people and their family and wanna put them in poverty = enemy!

A loser pope takes on Trump. A socialist globalist dope wants us flooded with chumps.

Pope is really in a hole he can't crawl out of now. This no-borders accuser isn't God, you know.

They make themselves exempt from the tyrannical rules they put on us. That's how evil kings focus.

Daily disappointment for 8 years now gets worse as we're invaded by opposite values triggering fear.

AMERICANS WANT THE BORDER SECURED!

America wants the border to be secured. Until then, their distrust of government won't ever be cured.

America is being dominated by global interests who've conquered the whole world and we're the last.

Globalism is totalitarianism--that's why it's so frightening. It's tyranny vs. creativity--the enlightening.

Taking our guns as they flood us with foes. This is worse than history's tyrants--as low as it goes!

What are we going to do? Illegal invaders are breaking into homes and chopping our heads off too.

AFFINITY OR MISERY

God step in and save America now. These aren't children but grown men crossing our borders--disallow!

It's not so much the police but the globalists behind it, but they want this division in America to trash it.

The endgame is to agitate minorities then discard them. Top dogs become bottom to their chagrin.

Become more protective than ever. Other cultures are entering in, they don't think like us about Rover.

With distant socialist government over us, it's hell. They don't care what you want--kids gettin us killed.

The globalists want us all queer. It's part of the eugenics depopulation plan, so they say "it's superior".

Globalists know if we're demoralized we're easy to control. Turning kids into pervs/sluts is their goal.

The right to invade my home/take it over: communism. The right to anything else I've got: socialism.

ISLAM AND THE BRUTISH CARNAL MAN

Islam appeals to ignorant, brutish, carnal men and spreads not by gospel or grace but the power of the sword. Aquinas

"Mohammad seduced people by promises of carnal pleasure and gave free rein to it, appealing to people of limited wisdom." Aquinas

They want Wash DC's arrogance to topple them--so the mega-globalist empire can *replace* them.

Soros and the super-left (hoarders) are behind global destabilization and all recently imploded borders.

Trillions in no-bid contracts destabilizing the world: Governments should be feared by every boy and girl.

AFFINITY OR MISERY

They should send "surplus tanks" back to Iraq--eliminate ISIS threat which will come here, in fact.

Stop being naive and see the whole plan. it goes way beyond petty notions of gov--see the con man.

As blind victims we've been taken over by foreign banking cartels following a total eugenics system.

The elites refuse to take GMO vaccines/foods. Yet they make us take them and eat them, dudes.

Regarding ISIS, the doves have become major hawks! Good--the denial and complacency really sux.

The kids wanted socialist Sanders cuz they never had Civics (to be specific) about things that matter.

They just wanted free stuff so they loved his guff but so dangerous if he had gotten in—woulda been rough.

Idiot college kids take it out on the middle class who employ people not the globalists who are evil.

Americans are spoiled with decency relative to the third world where it doesn't exist (like the socialists).

Rubio is the billionaire toy-boy. We didn't give in to this open borders politically correct ploy!

TRUMPISM EXPLODING ACROSS THE WORLD

The Trump phenomenon is occurring all over the world! Nationalism is arising along with God's word.

What PC is all about: (1) Break our will, to (2) accept foreign domination and that means globalism.

Elites are pushing disease, crime and terror being allowed into our country-- and it's happening abruptly.

AFFINITY OR MISERY

Why are billionaires coming against Trump? Cuz he can't be controlled and will come against them--hah.

Can't wait to see Trump collude with Putin cuz they're both real and Christian: to globalists, frightenin'

It's a global takeover involving everyone from Reid to DeCaprio and global warming's the first show.

Illegals voting: more lawlessness in this global takeover by calling us racist if we don't go for it.

Thought horrible: Suddenly he'll alert 10,000 sleeper cells who will surge while we're disabled.

We love Mexico but they're killing us at trade and killing us at the border so we want no more.

Treason came against us daily as he gave away our home and peace to our enemies, without remedy.

We can defeat globalism by nationalism! We are allowed to be proud of our Americana again.

TRUMP IS BREAKING HOAXES LIKE TPP

Trump is breaking the hoax of things like TPP: signing ourselves away to scams and global slavery.

Because they want a free lunch the people give into social engineering--like a technocratic sponge.

It's making us poor, sick and dumb--the technocratic revolution is worse than the tyranny of Marxism.

The under-thirties think socialism's okay, showing how dumb they are--the uneducated will be prey.

The GOP is panicking cuz soon they'll be on the outside looking in! Globalist gophers = trash bin.

AFFINITY OR MISERY

Until they realize Islam is a political system masquerading as religion they are never able to see 'em.

We're dragged down thinking about foes rather than the assured victory by our Father: He who knows!

Islam is a political system that conquers through rape, murder and taking slaves--and thus the Crusades.

It's as clear as the existence of gravity but still we're told "don't believe your lying eyes"--rise up, be bold!

We have a right to not feel fear but still they let them in against our will and in sheer terror.

Centralized global control is: picking winners and losers and making us poor.

Their plan: Start wars in other countries so that a massive relocation substitutes populations.

Your kids are taught to be global citizens in a collectivist, sexually reckless, "sustainable" world.

"Redistribute your wealth, open your borders, your nation stinks just like all you white man finks".

Multiculturalism says all cultures are equal. False: some are bad and many are dangerous, pal.

MULTICULTURALISM IS PERVERSION/COMMUNISM

Liberalism is now perversion and communism. It is not "liberalism" as we know it, but destruction.

They aren't true liberals as in era of JFK but cultural Marxists who have usurped the term for today.

A cruel people whom you don't know shall rule over you, if you hadn't thrown out you know who.

AFFINITY OR MISERY

Anti-Trump crowd flew communist flag during protest. Could it be any more clear re: these pests?

Obama shut down coal plants is what was helping China. Trump: Turn em back on or our end is final.

See Obama as a Krazy Kollege Kid. Understand: it's the same thing with a false Marxian narrative.

If it's so great to be Muslim why see it as a slur? It's these contradictions being illuminated, yes sir.

Germany under Merkel desires to play Miss Congeniality and wants Europe to pick up the tab, really?

Germany evicted an elderly people to accommodate migrants. Can you believe Merkel madness?

The biggest lie of multiculturalism is: all cultures are alike. How stupid--some are lethal, e.g. 3rd Reich.

Yay Putin--because ISIS is the number one problem on the planet, not the climate.

GOD KNOWS NO COWARDS

God knows no cowards who hide in the pew while crucial issues are eschewed--like borders any can go through.

One sign of American exceptionalism is how we love dogs while others have the hearts of logs.

Look at these sick creeps wearing the rainbow. New Age hypocrites and global warming, you know.

Who wants to be in a world where your dog is seen as food? The new world will be gross and crude, dude.

We were decent people but this stuff bringing us down must be rejected lest we become feeble weasels.

AFFINITY OR MISERY

They don't want that populism vetted--they want full entry and labeling us as "demented".

It is historical what's happening and super-creepy: A criminal takeover by the freaky and cheesy.

If you like the constitution you're a "bitter clinger" (to God and guns) and you will be targeted, son.

You say you don't go along with ISIS but you believe in the religion based on the Koran and it says this.

Islam has fed off the discontent of young black males in prisons--taking over America is their mission.

Youth think socialism is being "concerned with others". No--it's tyranny as government smothers.

Sudden Infant Death Syndrome is an auto-immune response--in most cases--coming from vaccines.

The elites get clean vaccines. We're not given the good stuff--our health's in their handcuffs.

CPS takes children like eggs from a hen. Taking the kids is the first stages in the growing communism.

SOCIALISM IS *ELITE* IN CONTROL NOT YOU

Socialism: an elite in control, a crumbling middle class and totally dependent and controlled mass.

Why would that president embrace the Muslim brotherhood when they've promised to kill us?

Whereas they feared us before, now (that we're obviously weak) they're on power trips galore.

The globalists want societal collapse while they're dug in poised to reorganize.

AFFINITY OR MISERY

Mass mental illness/cultural death is designed to mentally wound us so they can take control.

Learn about global government: it is unelected and will bring this system down.

We must stand together because in the end freedom triumphs over tyranny. Democrats said "don't evacuate"

The language of the left built the Islamophobic shield that harbors that evil, making us yield.

Trump and Putin are the stay against the expansionist, globalist, anti-Christian new wave.

Sick leftists celebrate hurricane as victory over conservative white Americans.

Thank God Trump stopped the rot. Nigel Farage

We've been called extremists, fascists, every name under the sun--but America's waking up/we got guns.

Trump was elected on a ticket and intends to implement it so thank God/look up with confidence.

After bringing jobs back/controlling illegal immigration he'll be most popular president ever imagined.

NATIONALISM IS PROPER AND NORMAL

Our lives were wrecked through global but re-establishing the nation state is right, proper and normal.

Only reason can break the grip of the murderous anti-Christ spirit. Stefan Molyneux

They were brainwashed against their will so they're wounded not merely horrible, but violent still.

AFFINITY OR MISERY

Globalism made poor countries or those they've made poor fodder for conquest so they hate our president.

Palermo now a mid-east slum, mafia declares war on migrant bums.

Communists cause the violence then blame the other side for it. For Stalinists and Alinskyites it's classic.

They call Trump racist cuz that's what communists do. I can't stand it and refuse to watch it too.

Taught to be politically correct, we have no immune system against cultural invasion and destruction.

Third World hardcore are always killing each other and since our men cower they just take us over.

TRUMPISM IS SPREADING QUICKLY

Trump got rid of ISIS, quick! He knew well the USA overwhelming power to lick.

One man can be a majority and suddenly clarify the whole world, as the old view is seen as failure.

A major re-alignment is happening poli-psychologically: fighting tyrants with out apology.

Foreign globalists say Trump is "Hitler" (the worst thing on earth) cuz he'll shut down the jerks.

Our country's been swallowed into global fascism. How far we've sunk--where is nationalism?

We've been taught all cultures are equal—what bull! Humaneness is a sliding scale.

The globalists use communism as a management system and it's happening here, amen.

QUISLING TRAITORS MUST GO

AFFINITY OR MISERY

Must get rid of all Quisling traitors like Boehner--contributing to the destruction of a nation disfavored.

They think we are inferior like animals, and also that we should be killed cuz we don't know Allah.

They're incompetent but then there's Donald Trump: not a globalist but what we the people want.

Trump's against globalism and unfair trade deals that sell us out, let alone bankster bail-outs.

The vampires who are sucking this country dry hate Trump even more as he takes us so high.

Trump's against foreign bureaucrats running our lives. He hates this globalist takeover and he will fight.

The Bush-Cruz Connection is clear so stay clear of this scammer unless you want open borders.

Cruz types are globalist operatives so blame Trump for the planned violence Hillary and Soros funded.

Many RINOS aren't about keeping US safe but ensuring the cheap labor pool of their donors, okay?

KEEP CHAOS TO BRING EM IN

Strong Cities Initiative of the U.N. Plan: Create chaos compelling foreign mercenaries to come in.

GOP insiders would rather have Hillary than Trump because at least she's globalist like them: scum.

The globalist system's like a swiss watch and Trump would be sand in the gears like a giant botch.

GOP are so globalist-bought they'd rather blow up the republicans for Hillary so abortion won't stop.

AFFINITY OR MISERY

Foreign occupation is being eased in through police departments. It's UN (global-controlled) government.

So China's good, Cuba's good but America is bad? No it's a globalism scheme and fad.

The globalists want total tyranny over us so align with Islam as their operating system.

Merkel screwed up because of self-loathing war guilt which makes her a crazy quilt.

The Cuban mafia leaders will never give up their riches and that's communism: vicious.

Communism is always fascism/riches at the top, no middle class then poverty nonstop.

Moderates who wanna change Islam are either killed or exiled. More religious, more riled.

Merkel opened the borders to Muslim males of military age-- progressives are not sage.

Socialist Merkel did it. Not Trump, racists, bigots nor xenophobes but a false dogma--so dump it.

DESTRUCTIVE OBSESSION WITH RACE: DIVERSITY

The diversity agenda is a destructive obsession with race.

Since they can't suddenly become smart and gentle they stay dumb and vicious but ask God for help.

Revitalization movements occurred all through history and were led by a charismatic leader always.

Revitalization movements in history changed society and governments after a long period of decline.

AFFINITY OR MISERY

A contagion of enlightenment has increased geometrically over the whole world. Thank you God!

Christianity is our original foundation. Our founders saw Islam as a political system of oppression, not a religion.

Islam invaded until the soft cuckolded males finally stood up. All through history this occurred--look it up.

Liberals are all about appeasement: If Muslims attack it's due to something we did to them.

"Capitulate to the Muslims or they'll attack" is the leftist's plan teamed with our enemies: fact.

Trump's the only nationalist in a field of globalists. Everything he says is about that, the gist.

A big fraud is taking place and they think you're so dumb you'll accept it/not save face.

They throw gays off buildings/stone women and still the left loves them, vermin.

There's only two things out there: Tyranny and conquest or liberty and freedom.

MASS MIGRATION TO LEVEL THE NATION

Trump is the only one against the policy of mass migration used to level our great nation.

I'm not bragging I just know what I'm talking about. The globalists want the bad in/good out.

Obama is a red diaper baby: son of a radical American communist and pornographer, okay?

Feminists conflate rape to "all" men while loving Islam--can you see the giant screwjob this is man?

AFFINITY OR MISERY

Despite globalism we must hold people accountable at the local level and then we get the devil.

He was handpicked to be the murderer of the truth and our national security: smooth.

Of course, dummy--we gotta have borders. Otherwise other countries will take us over.

ULTRA-RICH LOVE COLLECTIVISM

The ultra-rich are funding collectivism because they're exempt from it being offshore--treason.

Globalism: a bunch of special interests screwing over the nation state and that's why Trump is irate.

Sick of seeing this alliance between Wahhabists and the left. Are they crazy or just daft?

Just because all are hypnotized doesn't make it not true. It's happening and it's cruel.

A socialist is: a pile of horse manure that thinks it's smart. That's 60% of college kids--no heart.

French gays loved Le Pen--woulda been their savior from what's to come.

France failed cuz they're into fashion, trendiness, going along with the herd/being part of establishment.

FRENCH NOT CAPTURED ANYMORE!

It's not that the French are wimps, just captured by propaganda--but isn't it the same? It's not American.

In panic over growing nationalism worldwide the globalists rigged the election against patriot Le Pen.

They want world gov as it's eugenics--playing God, but moving into open they're seen as clods.

AFFINITY OR MISERY

We're all under stress. Only the dense don't feel this global mess. Pray for escape and God will bless.

The globalists want feminism cuz it breaks up families. Women in agreement just create tragedies.

Agenda 21 is moving to take all the land. That's just one part--better savor freedom while you can.

Beirut was the France of the East now France is the Beirut of the West.

Our subversive Frankenstein went to Cuba to pump up the dictator act or make it less of a fact.

Cubans are prisoners of the two biggest mafioso in the world: the Castro brothers were cold.

Army of darkness: a braindead zombie force bred by television and it is dangerous and crazy.

Spoiled rotten drug addicts in the NFL--just check their high crime rate if you have any doubts.

These are the enemy soldiers: the zombie force. Don't laugh at this, it is no farce.

The trade deals are the greatest treachery against our people since our beginnings--evil.

DEMOCRATS USE ACTORS/COMEDIANS

It's a victory for the elite but we're getting the word out. Democratic leader: Colbert the actor has clout?

How surrealistic to see France conquered by Germany again. Germany's head of the EU: Merkel.

Macron not an old lady fettish but a globalist plan to get the feminist vote-- every woman's dreams of such.

AFFINITY OR MISERY

The media promotes pure death, anti-free market and anti-family: Get offa that thing, really.

Hidden they had power but once totalitarians are revealed they begin to fall from their tower.

Our children are prepped to go to college and get into debt. Then they're socialists, all wet.

Traitors like Paul Ryan want a place at the table after selling us completely out till we're crippled.

We've been conquered by foreign multinational interests but who are also stinking perverts.

We're in the clutches of a big ol' mean snake. It's trying to swallow a bull and it's a big mistake.

They wanna make us slaves and mount our head on the wall and tell us we're obsolete/will fall.

They bring five million Jihadis in to attack--and when they do attack, I have to lose more liberty?

To pseudo-intellectual leftists: You're in a cult--the mere fact it's allied with Islam, you know it.

Goal: Flood nation states, get em fighting with each other, have no excellence with them over us.

The globalists are on power-mad trips with the info they've stolen from humanity--think of this.

GLOBALISTS USE PSYCH WARFARE

The globalists are using psych warfare to overthrow reality so you'll give in/let them win eventually.

Turning our world upside down by making us accept philosophical garbage and pure rubbish.

AFFINITY OR MISERY

They're bringing down the west by flooding us with the dregs saying it's for the best.

Paul Ryan is a globalist subversive like many others we trusted. Pay attention then get disgusted!

The RINOS have divided the country, destroyed its borders and empowered its enemies.

Friends and enemies are putting their country above ours, so we must defend the stripes and stars.

Globalism is communism which has never worked, leading to corruption and poverty (no perks).

In communism you're given the bare minimum--you get only what they decide to give, amen?

Myth of integration: Muslims in Europe are getting more radicalized with time, not less.

You can't give a free lunch and not put a wall around it. This is a sinking ship, think about it.

Concern over "Russian meddling" but not non-citizens voting: Typical of leftists, so contradictory.

Globalists create anarchy with control as the answer. They also keep secret their cures for cancer.

ELITES WANT US MAD AT COPS

The elites want us mad at the cops--they want them out and their guys in: the global police, a box.

Globalists seek to blend us together, destroying markers like flags while distracting with the weather.

The TransPacific Trade deal would've brought grinding poverty for all. No more Americans walking tall.

AFFINITY OR MISERY

We were a decent country but now we gotta tolerate such horrible things like beheadings.

Multiculturalism is basically just divide and conquer. It will never work but you think it's good/no fear?

They want consolidation so make order out of chaos by getting more control of the nation.

Send us their worse people but refusing the same--calling us "racists" like we're to blame.

This creeping Sharia is the biggest threat to western freedom but they can't see that, amen?

The most advanced countries are declining--going out of business. It's a holocaust but God will bless.

Globalism: The left is their takeover arm, but they use compliant people on the right as well.

I believe no man could fail to drop the bomb and look his countrymen in the face. Truman

Venezuela and other socialist paradises: "There is no rice, pasta or flour--only hunger".

MUSLIMS HATE DOGS LET ALONE CATS

What's going to happen to all the dogs and cats when animal-unfriendly immigrants come in?

Islam is the operating system for the new world order and you can see it happening, oh Lord.

It's individualism vs. collectivism and the latter is hell. I felt it in kindergarten, a communist smell.

Why is the left so affiliated with Islam? They kill gays and women but just another contradiction.

AFFINITY OR MISERY

We are invaded by millions but unaware since these are sleepers to later kill us, so prepare.

The Trojan horse is through the gate. No time to be irate, it's gonna ramp up to a terrible fate.

Why take it out on local police? Feds want that to bring in the UN due to the violence increase.

Never forget this election is for the children, or the alternative is hell on earth, longterm.

He wants the love of Muslims--their approval and respect--for population Jihad, a promise kept.

A nationalized police force is the globalists plan but they make it look like it solves racism, man.

Due to multiculturalism they don't know to prefer their own. Where has logic/common sense gone?

Multiculturalism is a disease destroying all cultures with a top elite defining what true culture is.

Vladimir: We hate (him and her). Can you join with Trump to be our visionary and hope to be freer?

God says to separate from evil. We are not "one" but through borders stay a sweet people.

DON'T TELL ME WE'RE THE SAME

Don't tell me we're on the same level. That's communism and it's only the new age devil.

Donald Trump loves dogs. He doesn't hate em like the Muslims cuz he's of the true God.

Venezuela wanted "equality" so ended up with absolutely nothing: Socialism ain't loving.

AFFINITY OR MISERY

Economic collapse from a centralized, interventionist economy and you want this here, a monstrosity?

Venezuelan violence is endemic to socialism--and Bernie/Hillary want to bring it here, like a prison.

Black Lives Matter has joined with ISIS, a catastrophe--but you know who created this crisis.

Millions of aliens are flooding in and they'll all vote democrat without voter ID laws--understand that?

You need photo ID to buy a gun, but not to vote? Even those aliens flooding in to slit our throats?

Jihad wins in dumb (tolerant) countries in a cultural suicide causing their own demise.

Unvetted refugees are flowing into small towns across the United States--we're scared and irate.

The shady criminal democrats are flooding us to turn America blue and we will be so blue!

Injections of vaccines with trojan horse additives to control populations.

Khan is working for criminals running government and Hillary and he makes money off of refugees.

The whore media and Obama clan is all about massive propaganda and denial about radical Islam.

THERE IS NO WAR ON WOMEN (IN THE WEST)

There is no "war on women" other than the Middle East. Racism too but we get this lie from the beast.

All you gotta do is restore local politics--power to the people will remove globalism's horrible evil.

AFFINITY OR MISERY

The dishonest press puts a false spin on everything, supported by the globalists for lying.

The evils of multiculturalism can now be seen. Degraded to the lowest and surrounded by fiends.

We're gonna kick the ass of ISIS. That's what Trump said and we feel relief as if it's an oasis.

Olympics: for the exceptional but due to socialism the starting speech says "we're all equal". bull!

Jihadis are bad for kids, women and dogs--they kill em. Now they invaded Italy but the mob'll get em.

Economic warfare (e.g. Venezuela) is a long term program and that's why it's so hard to turn it around.

American foreign policy was always based on human rights but no more-- and it's sad, it's a blight.

Zero tolerance for criminal aliens. That's Trumpism and I love it cuz it's nationalism.

It's Marxist New World Order crap that's being advanced all the time. Let em in and censure us while lying.

To make them self-deport simply turn off the spigot. Deport those in prison then vet all and mean it.

WHEN DOES ALTRUISM BECOME ROBBERY?

Where does selflessness end and communism begin? When does altruism become robbery and sin?

The criminal flood will instantly subside. He'll fire the prior, turn off the spigot and deport the snide.

It's a Shariah-based trojan horse meant to stifle all criticism of Islam--are you truckling to this ma'am?

AFFINITY OR MISERY

They marry children. They stone women. They kill dogs and you love em--or don't know about em?

We have an evil, sadistic, monstrous enemy and we must keep these killers out of our country.

You don't deport em you lure em to self-deport. That's the only way, make it about money/great import

When they bomb you, it's not a bombing. And when they stab you just wear a hijab and submit, crawling.

Their goal is to blow America up and make it in their image. They're superior (won't assimilate) and feel privileged.

He got the Chinese to do our dirty work in North Korea. He's not crazy he's a true genius I'll betcha.

Trump was elected on a ticket and intends to implement it so thank God and you can now be confident.

All agree Antifa is violent but do they see left's link to Islam is the entry to tyranny and the end?

Sharia--amputation for theft, stoning for adultery, death to homosexuals--must be banned in America.

Western countries built on a Christian understanding of the world protected boys and girls.

MULTICULTURALISM SINCE THE SIXTIES

Since the sixties we emphasized multiculturalism and lost our own roots--and became the caboose.

Flooding nations with immigrants is violent invasion and nothing less, and liberals make this mess.

In her book Hillary blamed 43 people or things for her loss: Classic psychopathy of the gross.

AFFINITY OR MISERY

Gobalist boytoys Macron, Obama, Trudeau hold the fate of whole nations in their dirty little hands.

Suddenly being surrounded by strangers is an example of God's wrath--terrible, terrifying, want a bath.

He promised to undo Obama's legacy and hadn't but now stopping "dreamers" creates havoc.

They never consider the people already here--adapt or leave.

Only low wage employers benefit, the rest of us are hurt by it.

Americans have the right to determine who comes to their country but the left calls that bigotry.

Why not just say you want open borders with no restrictions not all the other false elucidations.

Left doesn't believe in borders they'd let the whole world in even rapers.

Is it ok for anyone to come here illegally and stay? If that is the rule, what's it gonna be like, fools?

Multiculturalism is the biggest lie ever imposed on the West for all cultures are not alike.

You say if we don't placate them enough it's our fault when we're attacked? Insane, that's a fact.

Multiculturalism is being pushed as hatred for the white race and colleges are caving to this disgrace.

LEFTIST UNIVERSITIES HATE AMERICA

It almost doesn't matter if ISIS is here, the leftist universities hate America more--we've reason to fear.

The days of hating on America are coming to an end. They're cheering our Donald, America's best friend.

AFFINITY OR MISERY

The time of economic surrender is over as we enter a new industrial revolution like never seen before.

The left has become a vacuous, declining and decaying organization but even so they attack for the duration.

Liberals love free speech, as long as it's theirs. Anyone they disagree with and they're violent bears.

Dems don't wanna turn us loose and let us meet our destiny--but mount our head on the wall/make us unfree.

Go ahead and threaten, devil destiny--you can defeat this body but not the contagious ideas of liberty.

We're never sick of winning but we are sick of the left's whining about all the reasons they're declining.

Global warming is the left's golden key to turn the world to socialism and wealth redistribution, see?

Stop saying the American dream is dead when it's only just beginning. We're gonna explode soon, winning.

THE RUSSIAGATE SCAM

Anyone against globalism is called "Russian agent"

Setting a man on fire in a cage--it's all okay with the progressive vermin when they should feel rage.

These are antithetical cultures—they hate everything you love/cherish like your pets with fur.

World leaders hate Obama cuz he's a traitor to his own country. Anyone can see this, Putin primarily.

Have you seen Putin destroying Russia or traveling abroad putting his people down (like our clown)?

AFFINITY OR MISERY

Obama's involved with Pizzagate--child rape--priming us for Islam where that's basic: mean fate.

Are we gonna continue to deal with one crime after another, after another-- or realize we're in a war?

ISIS plan: Infiltrate the refugee system. The feds place em in the states who lose em in the slum.

FEDS place em in the states who don't know who they are. Preposterous to deny our rights/act as a czar.

This historical period evokes the entrepreneurial spirit. Now we can do our thing without fearing it.

A magic switch thrown when Trump got elected, signalling we're not laying down anymore, nor rejected.

Trump's hired world geniuses, top of their game, for we the people who no longer are ashamed.

Obama can't say Islamic but has no problem with saying Christian crusades. We've had it in spades.

LIBERALISM USED TO MEAN HUMANE

It doesn't mean what it used to--in the days of JFK. It's now a front for globalist communism, okay?

Muslim avoids jail for anally raping teen cuz he couldn't understand "no" and it's part of his culture, see?

Liberals love Jihad warriors. Yet if they dressed like that they'd be beaten to death by Hillary's donors.

Truth-tellers are called "haters"

Left's alliance with Islam will sour: Even gays like it but like a harlot in Arabia they'd be dead in hour.

AFFINITY OR MISERY

We're flooded. Better wake up peeps cuz it's happening overnight and we need Trump not duds.

I loved the area but it didn't love me. It was a constant curse so I strategically relocated to be free.

THE NEW RENAISSANCE IF HE'S BACK IN

Trump gets in and the New Renaissance is here!

Romney called Trump a "phony, a fraud and a con man". Good riddance Mitt you arrogant garbage can.

Mitt Romney was a choker in the key moment of the election against Obama (the commie robber).

Trump was a rock star at the Army-Navy game. Obama was there but ignored due to infamy: bad fame.

The CIA Russia finding is ridiculous--just another excuse. Donald Trump

Hack claim is perfect example of propaganda media. Newt Gingrich

Calling out corrupt media is "unhinged"

It's not the end, it's the beginning of the end. Winston Churchhill

Why do libs hate Russia? They covered Trump favorably in their news so the left wants war--makes us blue.

Since the failure of rationalization means self-incrimination, failure is avoided at all costs. pride or lost.

RATIONALIZATION DRIVES CULTURE WAR

Rationalization drives the culture war. Against God, it's based on desperation, increasing it's power more.

They only want recount in states lost by Hillary--not those won by by her through fraud (chicanery).

AFFINITY OR MISERY

When our man finally has power he's gonna clean house and speedily as these evils are all thrown out!

God will remove the evil in leadership and those who stand in the way of His agenda: Donald we love ya.

Obviously it's a power grab and they even admit that's what it is: Science shows temp hasn't risen one bit.

Pollution is worse where government controls the land. The cure for pollution: get government out, man.

America is not about learning slogans but entrepreneurship and with Common Core that's broken.

It's not for the "greater good" but rather total control: Understood, it is communism led by hoods.

"Peace" to globalists means submission—not fighting them anymore. Not world peace, they want war.

Commies know the people who are falling in with them are so stupid they can't trust em so they kill em.

It doesn't matter who the shooter is—blame the gun (or the truck)

It's a war between massive tyranny and the individual's freedom, justice and liberty and it's not pretty.

Political correctness from Soviet Union: lunatics with chips on shoulders running around bullying everyone.

GOAL OF NOW: TEN REGIONS/NO NATIONS

The goal of the NWO is to break up world into 10 regions. The block to this is our identity: nationalism.

It's a corporate democracy under world communism—we just escaped this by banishing Hillary Clinton.

AFFINITY OR MISERY

Obama began with an apology tour now a "me too" tour of the land, looking so silly following around The Man.

The leftist losers are frantic, continuing to put out insidious lies against Trump but no one buys it.

Enemy is melting down worse than we thought but we'll still strike back.

Globalization effecting us at very local levels, gotta block this devil.

It makes you sick seeing all the changes, imposed by an unelected body who are careless/deranged.

Talking lies, omitting or slanting facts is an attack on your country, Jack.

KEEP SMALL TOWNS INTACT

Must keep our small towns intact. Not succumb to globalists who wanna strip us of refinement/tact.

My favs are Bonanza and Big Valley. It's true Americana: strength, honor, liberty, individuality.

Many are cold-blooded, others are hot. Being dense some can practice their trade but most cannot.

They're bigger than we are: With the power and means their "pain compliance" is even used on teens.

Everyone thinks they're on the red carpet. FB gives that illusion as they seek fame: social harlots.

The "star": no different from any addict going down to turn around to become renowned.

If they're not against it they're for it--no lukewarm. It's a dividing line-- separation works like a charm.

THE CHIC WILL BE UP A CREEK

They act "tough" and "chic" but without worthy study they'll be up a creek cuz

AFFINITY OR MISERY

it's sick what they seek.

Give me a break! When those people become full of themselves it's all I can take: yikes—snakes.

They flit around to no good: the trendies: They talk like gangstas and it's all a fake (not truly friendly).

Merriment and enjoyment: God grants us this. But when all around is perversion, to God and Self it's a DIS!

Newspeak says my worst defects are who I am and so if you criticize them you're no friend.

They've stopped judging anything at all. That's made them psychotic zombies and soon they will fall.

If you're not syrupy sweet, if you don't smile, if you just live your life they'll say "she's filled with guile".

Un-geniuses follow the plan. They can't break out, they've sought approval since time began.

Avoid worthless and futile debate. You know you're right, you don't have to pick a bone with fate.

The ungodly are like flowers in a field, disappearing as smoke: Though they flourish, soon they're broke.

Only God gives self-esteem, not pumping ourselves up--for whatever you try you're still just a grub.

Since the female psyche screens out info from what they want to believe, they're easily deceived.

THE DUMB PUT THE SMART DOWN

The dumb put the smart down: they heckle, mimic and frown. Don't get rundown, you'll be renowned.

AFFINITY OR MISERY

Stop arguing with idiots. It'd be better to stay silent for it's too tedious (since they are oblivious).

You'd get more from Bonanza then enduring the news. Just know it gets worse then avoid the blues.

We're social animals but to the extent one is not, he's on a different walk: it's deep thought not empty talk.

When it comes to guns, women need em more. That's why I can't understand the fem-trendies I abhor.

Don't fret when the evil flourish for soon they'll be gone. Though a swan, soon they'll be a bug you step on.

The wicked are like the beauty of fields: soon they vanish. Though evil is clannish it's still demolished.

Though beautiful on the outside, on the inside they are (dead men's bones and evil) Jekyll and hyde.

To stay away from bad people, be a sleuth. They're often seen as the nicest and purist--that's the truth.

WELLNESS UPDATES

Money: I never made a penny but had a vision and had to fulfill that, NOW it's payoff so don't tell me man.

You say there's nothing on TV but what about Turner Classic Old Movies? Too generalizing.

Just found out cocktail shrimp is highest protein per and GLYCATION DEFENSE needed for allure.

It's not a life of toil but exaggerated sacrifice. I've been up all night and worked all day my whole life.

I couldn't stand the gnawing hunger/sense of insatiety from a high-carb low-fat/protein diet.

AFFINITY OR MISERY

The minute I took the cocktail shrimp I felt so much better and increasingly energetic days later.

Being a pescatarian solved the nausea problem I had with hunger and it made life so much easier.

WHAT AM I SUPPOSED TO EAT

We eat smoothies, dips and soups. Everything smooth all goes through and gets into the tissues too.

So you like rock n' roll but I like chill. I don't see how we can ever bridge that gap so goodbye still.

Prepare to be discovered. The work is done and you're pretty as heaven hon', get ready for fun.

How about this, lovely Lilliputian: When it comes to power, less is more as as it all clears.

Einstein said "Most Creative Energy Comes in Least Mass" and that one line meant everything to this lass.

Soups, smoothies, dips--how else would you do it? Eat a big steak or mac and cheese? No stick

Picasso and Frank Lloyd Wright did their best work in their 90's with only catnaps. You sleep too much.

Fast food effects are insidious and slow but add up to something that is not-you and crazy too.

I think it's all from God yet when Jesus said that they called him arrogant but Who else this good.

This ends a fifty year creative cycle I began in 1970. I was never paid but persevered anyway honey.

I was never paid chump change but am preparing for **ONE HUGE CHECK** cuz that's what I'm to expect.

100 KAREN KELLOCK BOOKS

AFFINITY OR MISERY
AGELESS CORNUCOPIA
AMERICA AWAKE!
AMERICA'S DAFT ERA
ARTS OF PALEO FASTING
AUTOPHAGY ON CHEATERS
BACKSTABBING NEUROTICS
BETRAYAL TRAUMA
BOOMERS AND BROKENNESS
BOOT ON NECK
CHAMPION GUIDES
COMMIE NUTHOUSE
COMMIES
COMMUNIST SPIRIT
CONTAGION OF MADNESS
CONTAGIOUS MADNESS
CULTURE CLASH BASHED
DAFT LEFT
DAILY FASTARIAN
DAM RATS
DIVERSITY IS CRUELTY
E-RACE WHITE
EVIL FREAKS (Beyond Gross)
THE END OR A BEND?
FEMALE BULLIES AND FEMI-NAZIS
FEMALE CARNALITY
FEMALE DUMB DOWN
FEMALE POWER DRIVE
FEMINISM AND RUIN 1 & 2
FIX FOR MISFITS
FOOLS & TRAMPS
FREEDOM SPEAKING
FRENEMY ENABLER
FRENEMY LIAR
FRENEMY THIEF
FRENEMY TRAITOR
TRENEMY TYRANT
GENIUS IS HELD DOWN
GLOBALISLAM
GOD USES THE FLAWED
HAZE OF THE LATTER DAYS

THE HERD IN WORDS
HIX POLITIX
HOW THEY RUINED US
JUST SKIP DINNER
LE FEMME AND THE COMMUNIST SPIRIT
LIBERAL CHAOS & ROT
LIBERAL DOUBLETHINK
LIBERAL GALL 1 & 2
LIBERAL SHOVE-DOWNS
LOCK YOUR GATE
LOSERS and Femme Fatales
MANUAL FOR SUPERIOR MEN
MODERN ART FROM HELL
MOSTLY FAKE
NOTES TO CHAMPS 1 & 2
OVERCOME FRENEMIES
PC MAKES US CRAZY
PEOPLE ARE CRUEL
PEOPLE PROBLEMS 1 & 2
PERSECUTED GENIUIS
POLI-PSYCH MYSTERIES
PRETENTIOUS SLOBS
QUEEN BEE
RED NEW DEAL
RETURNING TO FIRST NATURE
SEASON OF TREASON
SEPARATE MEANS HOLY
SOCIAL HYPNOTISM
SOLITUDE SOLUTION
SUPERCILIOUS
THE SCHOOLS SCREWED EM UP
TOAD TO PRINCE
TRIALS CYCLES
TRUMP VS. GROUP
TRUST IN TRASH
THE TRUTH ABOUT PEOPLE
UNDERHEANDEDLY CLEVER
WALK TALL WITHIN WALLS
WE'RE NOT ALL ONE
WINNERS SKIP DINNER
WORK OR SMERK

KAREN KELLOCK PH.D.

M.S. Political Science, San Diego State. Ph.D. in Psychology, University of California Irvine. Postdoctoral: UCI School of Medicine, Dept. of Psychiatry [NIMH Grants]. Developed the Debris Theory of Disease, a theory of system pathology in 120 books and 22 textbooks for the general public. The theory has a general formula: All disease is obstruction, all recovery is elimination, all success is attraction. The three obstructions are people, habit and food. Remove obstruction and snap to your goals, waiting in the wings.